A Kalmus Classic Edition

George Frideric
HANDEL

JUDAS MACCABAEUS

An Oratorio

for Soli, Chorus and Orchestra

CHORAL SCORE

K 06206

Kalmus

INDEX TO JUDAS MACCABÆUS.

PART THE FIRST.

JUDAS MACCABÆUS.

CHARACTERS REPRESENTED.

JUDAS MACCABÆUS.
SIMON, HIS BROTHER.

AN ISRAELITISH MESSENGER.
ISRAELITISH MEN AND WOMEN

ARGUMENT.

PART I.—Lamentations for the death of Mattathias (the father of Judas Maccabæus and Simon), by whom the Jewish people had been roused to resist the cruelties and oppressions of Antiochus Epiphanes, the Syrian King, in his attempt to suppress their religion and liberties.—The divine favour invoked.—Judas recognised as leader.—Appeal to the patriotism of the people, and their response.—The value of liberty.—Preparations for war.—Pious trust in God, and heroic resolve to conquer or die.

PART II.—Celebration of the victories gained over the armies of Apollonius the Governor of Samaria, and Seron the Deputy Governor of Cœlesyria; and the valour of Judas.—Renewal of war by a division of the Syrian army from Egypt, under Gorgias, and the despondency it occasions amongst the Israelites.—Judas again arouses the failing courage of the people, and they set out to meet the enemy.—Those who remain behind utter their detestation of the Heathen Idolatries, by which the Sanctuary at Jerusalem had been desecrated, and their determination only to worship the God of Israel.

PART III.—Feast of the dedication at Jerusalem, after Judas and his followers had recovered and restored the Sanctuary, and re-established the liberties of his country.—Return of Judas from his final victory over Nicanor and his confederates.—Celebration of peace, and national thanksgiving.

Part the First.

OVERTURE.

SCENE.—*Modin.*

ISRAELITES, *Men and Women, lamenting the death of* MATTATHIAS, *Father of* JUDAS MACCABÆUS.

CHORUS.

Mourn, ye afflicted children, the remains
Of captive Judah, mourn in solemn strains;
Your sanguine hopes of liberty give o'er;
Your hero, friend, and father is no more.

RECIT.—*Israelitish Man.*

Well may your sorrows, brethren, flow
In all th' expressive signs of woe;
    Your softer garments tear,
    And squalid sackcloth wear,
Your drooping heads with ashes strew,
And with the flowing tear your cheeks bedew.

Israelitish Woman.

Daughters, let your distressful cries
And loud lament ascend the skies;
    Your tender bosoms beat, and tear
    With hands remorseless, your dishevell'd
        hair:
For pale and breathless, Mattathias lies,
Sad emblem of his country's miseries.

DUET.

From this dread scene, these adverse pow'rs,
  Ah! whither shall we fly?
O Solyma, thy boasted tow'rs
  In smoky ruins lie!

CHORUS.

For Sion lamentation make
With words that weep and tears that speak.

RECIT.—*Simon.*

Not vain is all this storm of grief,
To vent our sorrows gives relief.
Wretched indeed; but let not Judah's race
Their ruin, with desponding arms, embrace;
Distractful doubt, and desperation,
Ill become the Chosen Nation,
Chosen by the great I AM,
The Lord of Hosts, who, still the same,
We trust will give attentive ear
To the sincerity of pray'r.

AIR.— *Israelitish Woman.*

Pious orgies, pious airs,
Decent sorrow, decent pray'rs,
Will to the Lord ascend, and move
His pity, and regain his love.

CHORUS.

O Father, whose Almighty pow'r
The heav'ns, and earth, and seas adore,
The hearts of Judah, thy delight,
In one defensive band unite,
And grant a leader bold and brave,
If not to conquer, born to save.

RECIT. ACCOMPANIED.—*Simon.*

I feel the Deity within,
Who, the bright Cherubin between,
  His radiant glory erst display'd.
To Israel's distressful pray'r
He hath vouchsaf'd a gracious ear,
  And points out Maccabæus to their aid.
Judas shall set the captive free,
And lead us on to victory.

AIR.

Arm, arm, ye brave; a noble cause,
  The cause of Heav'n, your zeal demands;
In defence of your nation, religion, and laws,
  The Almighty Jehovah will strengthen
    your hands.

CHORUS.

We come, we come, in bright array,
Judah, thy sceptre to obey.

RECIT.—*Judas.*

'Tis well, my friends; with transport I behold
The spirit of our fathers, famed of old
For their exploits in war;—Oh, may their fire
With active courage you, their sons, inspire;
  As when the mighty Joshua fought,
  And those amazing wonders wrought,
Stood still, obedient to his voice, the sun,
Till kings he had destroy'd, and kingdoms
  won.

AIR.

Call forth thy pow'rs, my soul, and dare
The conflict of unequal war:
Great is the glory of the conquering sword
That triumphs in sweet liberty restor'd.

RECIT.—*Israelitish Woman.*

To Heav'n's Almighty King we kneel,
For blessings on this exemplary zeal.
Bless him, Jehovah, bless him, and once more
To thy own Israel liberty restore.

AIR.

O Liberty, thou choicest treasure,
Seat of virtue, source of pleasure;
Life without thee knows no blessing,
No endearment worth caressing.

AIR.*

[Come ever smiling Liberty,
  And with thee bring thy jocund train;
For thee we pant and sigh, for thee
  With whom eternal pleasures reign.]

RECIT.*—*Israelitish Man.*

[O Judas, may these noble views inspire
All Israel with thy true heroic fire.]

AIR.*

['Tis Liberty! dear Liberty alone!
That gives fresh beauty to the sun;
That bids all nature look more gay,
And lovely life with pleasure steal away.]

DUET.*

[Come ever-smiling Liberty,
  And with thee bring thy jocund train;
For thee we pant and sigh, for thee
  With whom eternal pleasures reign.]

CHORUS.

Lead on, lead on, Judah disdains
The galling load of hostile chains.

All those Airs, &c., marked thus * are usually omitted.

RECIT.—*Judas.*

So will'd my Father, now at rest
In the eternal mansions of the blest:
" Can ye behold," said he, " the miseries
" In which the long-insulted Judah lies?
" Can ye behold their dire distress,
" And not, at least, attempt redress? "
Then faintly, with expiring breath,
" Resolve, my Sons, on liberty or death."

Accompanied.

We come, O see, thy sons prepare
The rough habiliments of war,
With hearts intrepid and revengeful hands,
To execute, O Sire, thy dread commands.

SEMI-CHORUS.

Disdainful of danger, we'll rush on the foe,
That thy pow'r, O Jehovah, all nations
may know.

RECIT.*—*Judas.*

[Ambition! if e'er honour was thine aim,
The glorious cause gives sanction to thy
claim.]

AIR.*

[No unhallow'd desire our breasts shall
inspire,
Nor lust of unbounded power;
But peace to obtain, free peace let us gain,
And conquest shall ask no more.]

RECIT.—*Judas.*

Haste we, my brethren, haste we to the field,
Dependant on the Lord, our strength and
shield.

CHORUS.

Hear us, O Lord, on Thee we call,
Resolv'd on conquest, or a glorious fall.

Part the Second.

SCENE.—*The same.*

The ISRAELITES *celebrating the return of*
JUDAS *from the victories over* APOLLONIUS
and SERON.

CHORUS.

Fall'n is the foe; so fall thy foes, O Lord,
Where warlike Judas wields his righteous
sword.

RECIT.*—*Israelitish Man.*

[Victorious hero! fame shall tell,
With her last breath, how Apollonius fell;
And all Samaria fled, by thee pursued
Through hills of carnage and a sea of blood;
While thy resistless prowess dealt around
With their own leader's sword the deathful
wound;
Thus, too, the haughty Seron, Syria's boast,
Before thee fell, with his unnumber'd host.]

AIR.*

[So rapid thy course is,
Not numberless forces
Withstand thy all-conquering sword;
Though nations surround thee,
No power shall confound thee,
Till freedom again be restored.]

RECIT.—*Israelitish Woman.*

Well may we hope our freedom to receive,
Such sweet transporting joys thy actions
give.

DUET AND CHORUS.

Sion now her head shall raise,
Tune your harps to songs of praise.

RECIT.—*Israelitish Woman.*

O let eternal honours crown his name,
Judas, first Worthy in the rolls of fame;
Say, " He put on the breast-plate as a giant,
" And girt his warlike harness about him.
" In his acts he was like a lion,
" And like a lion's whelp roaring for his
prey."

AIR.

From mighty kings he took the spoil,
And with his acts made Judah smile.
Judah rejoiceth in his name,
And triumphs in her hero's fame.

DUET AND CHORUS.

Hail, hail, Judea, happy land!
Salvation prospers in his hand.

RECIT.*—*Judas.*

[Thanks to my brethren: but look up to
Heav'n!
To Heav'n let all glory and all praise be
giv'n;
To Heav'n give your applause, nor add the
second cause,
As once your fathers did in Midian,
Saying, " The sword of God and Gideon."
It was the Lord that for his Israel fought,
And this our wonderful salvation wrought."]

AIR.*

[How vain is man who boasts in fight
The valour of gigantic might,
And dreams not that a hand unseen
Directs and guides this weak machine.]

ENTER AN *Israelitish Messenger.*

RECIT.—*Messenger.*

O Judas, O my brethren!
New scenes of bloody war
In all their horrors rise.
      Prepare, prepare,
Or soon we fall a sacrifice
To great Antiochus: From th' Egyptian
      coast
(Where Ptolomy hath Memphis and Pelu-
      sium lost)
He sends the valiant Gorgias, and commands
His proud victorious bands
To root out Israel's strength, and to erase
Ev'ry memorial of the sacred place.

AIR AND CHORUS.

Ah! wretched, wretched Israel! fall'n how
      low,
From joyous transport to desponding woe.

RECIT.—*Simon.*

Be comforted—Nor think these plagues are
      sent
For your destruction, but for chastisement.
Heav'n oft in mercy punisheth, that sin
May feel its own demerits from within,
And urge not utter ruin—Turn to God,
And draw a blessing from his iron rod.

AIR.

The Lord worketh wonders
      His glory to raise,
And still as he thunders,
      Is fearful in praise.

RECIT.—*Judas.*

My arms! against this Gorgias will I go.
The Idumean Governor shall know
How vain, how ineffective his design,
While rage his leader, and Jehovah mine.

AIR.

Sound an alarm—your silver trumpets sound,
And call the brave, and only brave around.
Who listeth, follow — to the field again—
Justice, with courage, is a thousand men.

CHORUS.

We hear, we hear the pleasing dreadful call;
And follow thee to conquest—if to fall,
For laws, religion, liberty, we fall.
      [*Exit Judas with the Army.*

RECIT.*—*Simon.*

[Enough! to Heav'n we leave the rest,
Such gen'rous ardour firing ev'ry breast,
We may divide our cares.
The field be thine, O Judas, and the
      Sanctuary mine.
For Sion, holy Sion, seat of God,
In ruinous heaps is by the heathen trod;
Such profanation calls for swift redress,
If e'er in battle Israel hopes success.]

AIR.*

[With pious hearts, and brave as pious,
O Sion, we thy call attend,
Nor dread the nations that defy us,
God our defender, God our friend.]

RECIT.*—*Israelitish Man.*

[Ye worshippers of God!
Down, down with the polluted altars, down;
Hurl Jupiter Olympus from his throne,
Nor reverence Bacchus with his ivy crown
And ivy wreathed rod!
Our fathers never knew him, or his hated
      crew,
Or, knowing, scorn'd such idol vanities.]

Israelitish Woman.

No more in Sion let the virgin throng,
Wild with delusion, pay their nightly song
To Ashtoreth, yclep'd the Queen of Heav'n;
Hence to Phœnicia be the goddess driv'n;
Or be she, with her priests and pageants,
      hurl'd
To the remotest corner of the world;
Ne'er to delude us more with pious lies.

AIR.

Wise men, flatt'ring, may deceive you
      With their vain mysterious art;
Magic charms can ne'er relieve you,
      Nor can heal the wounded heart.
But true wisdom can relieve you,
      Godlike wisdom from above;
This alone can ne'er deceive you,
      This alone all pains remove.

DUET.—*Israelitish Woman.*

O never, never bow we down
To the rude stock, or sculptur'd stone:
But ever worship Israel's God,
Ever obedient to his awful nod.

CHORUS.

We never, never will bow down
To the rude stock, or sculptur'd stone
We worship God, and God alone.

Part the Third.

SCENE I.—*Mount Sion.*

ISRAELITISH PRIESTS, &c., *having recovered the Sanctuary.*

AIR.—*Priest.*

Father of Heav'n, from thy eternal throne,
Look with an eye of blessing down,
While we prepare, with holy rites,
To solemnize the Feast of Lights.
And thus our grateful hearts employ,
    And in thy praise
    This altar raise
With carols of triumphant joy.

RECIT. ACCOMPANIED.—*Israelitish Man.*

See, see yon flames, that from the altar broke,
In spiry streams pursue the trailing smoke;
The fragrant incense mounts the yielding air,
Sure presage that the Lord hath heard our
    pray'r.

RECIT.—*Israelitish Woman.*

O grant it, Heav'n, that our long woes may
    cease,
And Judah's daughters taste the calm of
    peace;
Sons, brothers, husbands, to bewail no more,
Tortur'd at home, or havock'd in the war.

AIR.

So shall the lute and harp awake,
    And sprightly voice sweet descant run,
Seraphic melody to make,
    In the pure strains of Jesse's Son.

RECIT.*—*Israelitish Messenger.*

[From Capharsalama, on eagle wings I fly,
With tidings of impetuous joy!
Came Lysias, with his host array'd
In coat of mail; their massy shields
Of gold and brass flash'd lightning o'er the
    fields,
While the huge tow'r-back'd elephant dis-
    play'd
A horrid front; but Judas, undismay'd,
Met, fought, and vanquish'd all the rageful
    train.
Yet more, Nicanor lays with thousands slain;
The blasphemous Nicanor, who defied
The living God, and in his wanton pride
A public monument ordained
Of victories yet ungained.

But lo! the conqueror comes; and on his
    spear,
To dissipate all fear,
He bears the vaunter's head and hand,
That threaten'd desolation to the land.]

SCENE II.—*Near Jerusalem.*

ISRAELITISH YOUTHS AND MAIDENS *meeting* JUDAS *on his return from the victory over* NICANOR.

SEMI-CHORUS.

See the conquering hero comes,
Sound the trumpets, beat the drums;
Sports prepare, the laurel bring,
Songs of triumph to him sing.
See the godlike youth advance,
Breathe the flutes and lead the dance;
Myrtle wreaths and roses twine,
To deck the hero's brow divine.

CHORUS.

See the conquering hero comes,
Sound the trumpets, beat the drums;
Sports prepare, the laurels bring,
Songs of triumph to him sing.

A MARCH.

SOLO AND CHORUS.

Sing unto God, and high affections raise
To crown this conquest with unmeasur'd
    praise.

RECIT.*—*Judas.*

[Sweet flow the strains that strike my feasted
    ear;
Angels might stoop from Heav'n to hear
The comely song we sing
To Israel's Lord and King.
But pause awhile: due obsequies prepare
To those who bravely fell in war.
To Eleazar special tribute pay;
Through slaughter'd troops he cut his way
To the distinguish'd elephant, and, 'whelm'd
    beneath
The deep-stabb'd monster,
Triumph'd in a glorious death.]

AIR.*

[With honour let desert be crown'd,
The trumpet ne'er in vain shall sound,
But all attentive to alarms
The willing nations fly to arms,
And conquering, or conquer'd, claim the
    prize
Of happy earth, or far more happy skies.]

SCENE III.—*Jerusalem, a Public Place.*

ISRAELITES *meeting* EUPOLEMUS, *the Jewish Ambassdor to Rome.*

RECIT.—*Eupolemus.*

Peace to my countrymen, — Peace and
  liberty;
From the great Senate of Imperial Rome,
With a firm league of amity, I come.
Rome, whate'er nation dare insult us more,
Will rouse, in our defence, her veteran pow'r,
And stretch her vengeful arm by land or sea,
"To curb the proud, and set the injur'd free."

CHORUS.

To our great God be all the honour giv'n,
That grateful hearts can send from earth to
  heav'n.

RECIT.—*Israelitish Woman.*

Again to earth let gratitude descend,
Praiseworthy is our hero and our friend:
Come my fair daughters, choicest art bestow,
To weave a chaplet for the victor's brow;
And in your songs for ever be confess'd
The valour that preserv'd, the power that
  bless'd.
Bless'd you with hours, that scatter as they
  fly,
Soft, quiet, gentle love, and boundless joy.

DUET.—*Israelitish Women.*

O lovely Peace, with plenty crown'd,
Come spread thy blessings all around,
Let fleecy flocks the hills adorn,
And valleys smile with wavy corn,
Let the shrill trumpet cease, nor other sound
But nature's songsters wake the cheerful
  morn.

AIR.—*Simon.*

Rejoice, O Judah, and in songs divine,
With Cherubin and Seraphin harmonious
  join.

CHORUS.

HALLELUJAH! AMEN.
Rejoice, O Judah, and in songs divine,
With Cherubin and Seraphin harmonious
  join.

No. 1.

OVERTURE.

BELWIN MILLS PUBLISHING CORP.
PRINTED IN U.S.A.

No. 1.   CHORUS.—MOURN, YE AFFLICTED CHILDREN.

6

No. 2   Recit.—WELL MAY YOUR SORROWS.

ISRAELITISH MAN.

Well may your sorrows, breth'ren, flow, In all th'ex-pressive signs of woe; Your

soft-er garments tear, And squalid sack-cloth wear; Your drooping heads with ashes

ISRAELITISH WOMAN.

strew, And with the flow-ing tear Your cheeks be-dew. Daughters, let

your dis-tress-ful cries, And loud lament, ascend the skies; Your ten-der bo-soms

beat and tear With hands re-morseless your dishevell'd hair. For pale and

breathless Mat-ta-thi-as lies; Sad em-blem of his country's mi-se-ries!

No. **3**   Duet.—FROM THIS DREAD SCENE.

ANDANTE
E
STACCATO.

TREBLE.

TENOR (8ve. lower.)

From this dread scene, these adverse pow'rs, Ah! whither shall we

From this dread

fly? Ah! whither shall we fly? O So-ly-ma, Ah!.. whither shall we fly?

scene, these ad-verse .. pow'rs, Ah! whither shall we fly! Ah! whither shall we

fly? O So-ly-ma, from this dread scene, these ad-verse

O So-ly-ma, Thy boasted tow'rs in smo - -

pow'rs, Ah! whi-ther shall we fly? Ah! whi-ther shall we fly? From this dread

- - ky ru - ins lie, in smo - - -

scene, O So-ly-ma, Thy boast-ed tow'rs

- - - ky ru - ins lie. From this dread scene, these

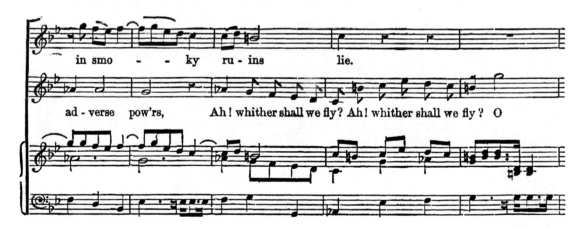

in smo - - ky ru - ins lie.

ad - verse pow'rs, Ah! whither shall we fly? Ah! whither shall we fly? O

O So-ly-ma, Thy boast-ed tow'rs in smo-ky ru - ins

So-ly-ma, O So - ly-ma, Thy boast-ed tow'rs

So - ly - ma, Thy boast - ed tow'rs in smo - ky ru - - ins lie.

So - ly - ma, Thy boast - ed tow'rs in smo - ky ru - - ins lie.

Tempo primo.

No. 4   CHORUS.—FOR SION LAMENTATION MAKE.

Larghetto e un poco piano.

ACCOMP.

Un poco piano.

TREBLE.   *Poco piano.*

For Si - on la - men - ta - - tion make,

ALTO.   *Poco piano.*

For Si - on la - men - ta - - tion make,

TENOR. (8ve lower.)

Poco piano.

For Si - on la - men - ta - - tion

BASS.   *Poco piano.*

For Si - on la - men - ta - - tion make,

Poco piano.

15

No. 5   RECIT.—NOT VAIN IS ALL THIS STORM OF GRIEF.

Air.—PIOUS ORGIES, PIOUS AIRS.

love. Pi-ous or-gies, pi-ous airs, De-cent sor-rows, de-cent pray'rs,

Will to the Lord ascend, and move his pi-ty, his pi-ty and re - gain his

love.

No. 7 CHORUS.—O FATHER, WHOSE ALMIGHTY POW'R.

LARGHETTO.

O Fa - ther, whose al - migh - ty pow'r

O Fa - ther, whose al - migh - ty pow'r

O Fa - ther, whose al - migh - ty pow'r

O Fa - ther, whose al - migh - ty pow'r

The heav'ns and earth, the heav'ns and earth, and

The heav'ns and earth, the heav'ns and earth, and

The heav'ns and earth, the heav'ns and earth, and

The heav'ns and earth, the heav'ns and earth, and

seas a-dore! The

seas a - dore! The

seas a - dore! The

seas a - dore! The

hearts of Ju — dah, thy de - light, In one de - fen - sive

hearts of Ju — dah, thy de - light, In one de - fen - sive

hearts of Ju — dah, thy de - light, In one de - fen - sive

hearts of Ju — dah, thy de - light, In one de - fen - sive

band u - - nite.

band u - - nite.

band u - - nite.

band u - - nite.

Allegro.

Allegro.

Allegro.

And grant a lead-er bold and brave, If not to con-quer, born to

Allegro.

8ves.

And grant a lead-er bold and brave, If not to con-quer, born to

save.   And grant a lead-er bold   and   brave, If not to con-quer,

No. **8**   Recit. (Accomp.)—I FEEL THE DEITY WITHIN.

No. **9**   Air.—ARM, ARM, YE BRAVE.

No **10**   Chorus.—WE COME, IN BRIGHT ARRAY.

-ray,   in bright ar - ray,   We come, we come,   in bright ar - ray,

-ray,   in bright ar - ray,   We come, we come,   in bright ar - ray,

-ray,   in bright ar - ray,   We come, we come,   in bright ar - ray,

-ray,   in bright ar - ray,   We come, we come,   in bright ar - ray,

Ju - dah,   Ju - dah,   Ju - dah,   Ju - dah, thy scep - tre, thy

Ju - dah,   Ju - dah,   Ju - dah,   thy scep - tre

Ju - dah,   Ju - dah   Ju - dah,   Ju - dah, thy scep - tre

Ju - dah,   Ju - dah,   Ju - dah,

scep - - - tre to . . o - bey

to o - bey, . . to . . o - bey.

Ju - dah, thy scep - tre to . . o - bey.

Ju - dah, thy scep - tre to o - bey.

8ves.

No. 11 RECIT.—'TIS WELL, MY FRIENDS,

JUDAS MACCABÆUS.

VOICE.

'Tis well, my friends; with transport I behold The spi-rit of our fathers, fam'd of

ACCOMP.

old For their exploits in war. Oh! may their fire With active courage you their sons in-

- spire: As when the mighty Joshua fought, And those amazing wonders wrought; Stood still,   o -

- - be-dient   to his voice, the sun,   'Till kings he had de-stroy'd,   and kingdoms won.

No. **12**   AIR.—CALL FORTH THY POWERS.

JUDAS MACCABÆUS.

VOICE.

Allegro.

Call forth thy pow'rs, my soul, and

ACCOMP.

Allegro.

Voice.

dare,   Call forth thy pow'rs, my soul, and dare   The con - flict, the

conflict of un-e - - qual war, ...   the

conflict of un - e - qual war. Call forth thy pow'rs, my

soul, and dare, ... and dare the con-flict of un -

- e - qual war, ... and dare the

con-flict of un - e - qual war.

Great is the glo-ry of the conqu'ring sword, of the con-qu'ring

sword, That triumphs in sweet li - berty restor'd. That tri - - umphs in sweet

li - ber-ty re-stor'd,   in sweet li - ber -ty   re-stor'd.

Call forth   thy pow'rs,   my soul,   and   dare,

Call forth thy pow'rs, my soul, and dare,   Call forth thy pow'rs, my soul, and

dare   The conflict,   the   conflict of un - e - - - - qual war, ...

. . . .   and dare   The conflict of un - e - qual

war.

No. 13 RECIT.—TO HEAVEN'S ALMIGHTY KING WE KNEEL.

To Heav'n's Al - migh - ty King we kneel, For blessings on this ex - em - pla - ry zeal. Bless him, Je - ho - vah, bless him, and once more To thy own Is - ra - el li - ber - ty re - store.

No. 14 AIR.*—O LIBERTY! THOU CHOICEST TREASURE.

O li - ber - ty! thou choicest treasure; Seat of vir - tue, source of plea-sure, Life with- out thee knows no blessing, No en - dearment worth caress-ing No endearment worth caress -

ing, no en-dear-ment worth ca-ress-ing.

Seat of vir-tue, source of pleasure; O! O liberty! thou choicest

trea-sure, Seat of vir-tue, source of plea-sure; Life without thee knows no

bless-ing, no endearment worth ca-ressing, no en-dearment, no endearment worth ca-ress -

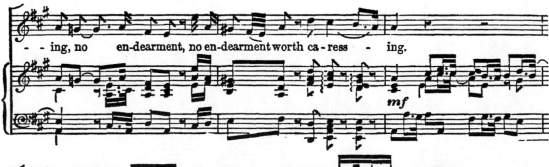

- - ing, no en-dearment, no en-dearment worth ca-ress - ing.

No. **15**   AIR.—COME, EVER SMILING LIBERTY.

No. 16 RECIT.—O JUDAS, MAY THESE NOBLE VIEWS INSPIRE.

ISRAELITISH MAN.

O Ju-das! may these noble views in-spire All Is-ra-el with thy true he-ro-ic fire.

No. 17 AIR.—'TIS LIBERTY.

Larghetto.

'Tis Li - - berty! dear Li-berty alone! That

gives . . fresh beau - - ty to . . the sun, That gives fresh beau-ty

to . . the sun. 'Tis Li - berty! 'Tis

Li - - ber-ty dear Li-ber-ty a-lone! That

And lovely life with pleasure steal a-way.

No. **18**　　DUET.—COME, EVER SMILING LIBERTY.

1st TREBLE
Come, e-ver smil-ing Li-berty, come, smil-ing Li-ber-ty

2nd TREBLE
Come, e-ver smiling Li-berty, smil-ing Li-ber-ty,

ACCOMP.

And with thee bring thy jocund train, with thee bring thy jo-cund train,

And with thee bring thy jocund train, with thee bring thy jo-cund train,

Come, e-ver - smil-ing Li-ber-ty,

Come, e-ver-smiling Li-ber-ty,

For thee we pant, and sigh for thee, . . and sigh for thee,

For thee we pant, and sigh for thee, For thee we pant, and sigh for thee,

With whom e - ter - nal plea - sures reign. Come, e - ver . . smil - ing Li - ber - ty,

With whom e - ter - nal plea - sures reign.

With whom e - ter - - - nal,

Come, e - ver smil - ing Li - ber - ty, With whom e - ter - - - nal,

with whom e - ter - nal plea - sures reign.

with whom e - ter - nal plea - sures reign.

No. **19** Chorus.—LEAD ON, LEAD ON.

Ju - dah disdains, Ju - dah dis-dains the gall-ing load of hos - tile

- -dains the gall - ing load of hos - tile chains, of hos - - tile

- -dains the gall - ing, gall - ing, gall - ing load, the gall-ing load of hos - tile

Ju - dah disdains the gall - ing, gall - ing load, the gall-ing load of hos - tile

chains. Lead

chains, Ju - dah dis-dains the gall - ing load of hos - tile chains. Lead

chains, Ju - dah dis-dains the gall - ing load of hos - tile chains. Lead

chains, Ju - dah dis-dains the gall - ing load of hos - tile chains. Lead

on, lead on, Ju - dah dis - dains the gall - ing load of hos - tile

on, lead on, Ju - dah dis - dains the gall - ing load of hos - tile

on, lead on, Ju - dah dis - dains the gall - ing load of hos - tile

on, lead on, Ju - dah dis - dains the gall - ing load of hos - tile

-dains, Ju-dah dis-dains the gall-ing load of hos-tile chains.

-dains, Ju-dah dis-dains the gall-ing load of hos-tile chains.

-dains, Ju-dah dis-dains the gall-ing load of hos-tile chains.

-dains, Ju-dah dis-dains the gall-ing load of hos-tile chains.

No. **20** RECIT.—SO WILL'D MY FATHER, NOW AT REST.

JUDAS MACCABÆUS.

VOICE.

So will'd my Father, now at rest In the e-ternal mansions of the blest;

ACCOMP.

"Can ye be-hold," said he, "the mi-se-ries In which the long in-sult-ed Ju-dah

lies? Can ye be-hold their dire distress, And not, at least, attempt redress?" Then

faintly, with ex-pir-ing breath, "Resolve my, sons, on li-ber-ty or death!" We

(Accompanied.)

(Accompanied.)

come, we come; Oh see, thy sons pre - pare The rough ha -

- bi - li-ments of war, With hearts in - tre - pid, and revengeful hands, To

ex - e - cute, O sire! thy dread commands.

No. **21** Chorus.*—DISDAINFUL OF DANGER.

Accomp. *Allegro.*

Alto. ‰ *1st Time as a Trio.*

Tenor. (8ve lower.) ‰ *1st Time as a Trio.*

Dis - dain - ful of

Bass. ‰ *1st Time as a Trio.*

Dis -

‰ *1st Time as a Trio.*

8ves.

Dis - dain - ful of dan - ger, we'll rush on the
dan-ger, we'll rush on the foe, on the foe, Dis - dain - ful of
- dain-ful of dan - ger, we'll rush on the foe, Dis - dain - ful of

foe, we'll rush on the foe, Dis - dain-ful of dan - ger, we'll rush on the
dan - ger, we'll rush on the foe, we'll rush on the foe,
dan - ger, we'll rush on the foe, Dis - dain - - - - -

8ves.

foe, we'll rush on the foe, we'll rush on the foe, Dis -
Dis - dain - ful of dan - ger, we'll rush on the foe, Dis -
- ful of dan - - - - - - - ger, Dis -

dain-ful we'll rush on the foe,   That thy   pow'r, O Je -

dain-ful we'll rush on the foe,   That thy   pow'r, O Je -

dain-ful we'll rush on the foe,   That thy   pow'r, O Je -

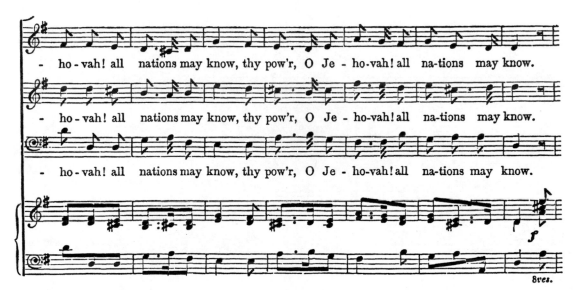

ho - vah! all   nations may know, thy pow'r, O Je - ho-vah! all na-tions may know.

ho - vah! all   nations may know, thy pow'r, O Je - ho-vah! all na-tions may know.

ho - vah! all   nations may know, thy pow'r, O Je - ho-vah! all na-tions may know.

Dis - dainful of

danger we'll rush on the foe, we'll rush on the foe, on the foe, . . Dis -

Dis-dain-ful of dan-ger, we'll rush on the foe, we'll rush on the

Dis -

- dain-ful of dan-ger, Disdain-ful of dan-ger, we'll

foe, Disdain-ful of dan-ger, Dis-dain-ful of dan-ger, we'll

- dain - - - - - - ful of dan-ger, we'll

8ves.

rush on the foe, dis - dain-ful we'll rush on the foe,

rush on the foe, dis - dain-ful we'll rush on the foe,

rush on the foe, dis - dain-ful we'll rush on the foe,

na - tions may know, That thy pow'r, O Je - ho - vah! all nations may know.

na - tions may know, That thy pow'r, O Je - ho - vah! all nations may know.

na - tions may know, That thy pow'r, O Je - ho - vah! all nations may know.

No. **22** RECIT.—AMBITION! IF E'ER HONOUR WAS THINE AIM.

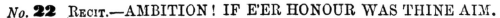

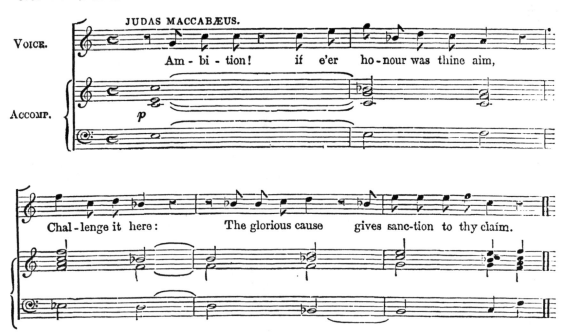

JUDAS MACCABÆUS.

VOICE.

Am - bi - tion! if e'er ho - nour was thine aim,

ACCOMP.

Chal - lenge it here: The glorious cause gives sanc - tion to thy claim.

No. **23**   AIR.—NO UNHALLOW'D DESIRE.

ACCOMP.

No, no un-hal-low'd de - sire Our breasts shall in - spire;

No, Nor lust of un - bound-ed pow'r, Nor lust of un-bound - ed

pow'r; No, no un - hallow'd de-sire Our breast shall in - spire, Nor

lust of unbound-ed pow'r, Nor lust of un-bound - ed pow'r, . . .

Nor lust of un-bound-ed

pow'r:

But peace to ob·tain, Free peace let us gain, And con-quest shall

ask no more, . . . no more, no more, And

conquest shall ask . . no more.

But peace t'ob·tain, Free peace let us gain, And

conquest shall ask no more. And con-quest shall ask no more, . . no

more,   no more,   no more, . . .

And

conquest shall ask no more,   But peace . . to ob - tain,   Free

peace . . let us gain,   And con - quest shall ask . . no more.

mf

No. **24**   Recit.—HASTE WE, MY BRETHREN.

Haste we, my brethren, haste we to the field; Dependent on the Lord, our strength and shield.

p

No. **25**   Chorus.—HEAR US, O LORD!

on conquest, on conquest, or a glo - rious, glo-rious fall.

on conquest, on conquest, or a glo - rious, glo-rious fall.

on conquest, on conquest, or a glo - rious, glo - rious fall.

on conquest, on conquest, or a glo - - - rious, glo - rious fall.

Hear us, O Lord! on Thee, . . O Lord! on Thee we call; Resolv'd on conquest,

Hear us, O Lord! on Thee, O Lord! on Thee we call; Resolv'd on conquest,

Hear us, O Lord! on Thee, O Lord! on Thee we call; Resolv'd on conquest,

Hear us, O Lord! on Thee, O Lord, on Thee we call; Resolv'd on conquest,

or a glo - rious fall.

or a glo rious fall.

or a glo - rious fall.

or a glo - rious fall.

8ves.

PART THE SECOND.

Chorus.—FALL'N IS THE FOE.

Fall'n is the foe, Fall'n is the foe; so fall thy foes, so fall thy foes, O Lord!

Fall'n is the foe, Fall'n is the foe; so fall thy foes, so fall thy foes, O Lord!

-- teous, righteous sword, where war-like Judas wields his righteous sword, his right-teous

wields his righ - - teous sword, his right-teous, righ - - teous

Where warlike Ju - - das wields his right - teous, righ - - teous

sword, his righteous sword.

Where warlike Ju - - das wields his righ - - - - - - teous

sword, his righteous sword, his righteous sword, Where warlike Judas wields his righ - - teous

sword.

Where warlike Ju - - das wields his right-teous

Fall'n is the foe,

Where warlike Ju - das wields his righ - teous

sword.

Fall'n is the foe, where warlike Judas wields his

sword.

Fall'n is the foe; so

sword.

Fall'n is the foe; so fall thy foes, O Lord!

Fall'n, Fall'n is the foe; so fall thy foes, O Lord! so

Fall'n, Fall'n is the foe; so fall thy foes, O Lord! so

Fall'n, Fall'n is the foe; so fall thy foes, O Lord! so

Fall'n, Fall'n is the foe; so fall thy foes, O Lord! so

fall thy foes, O Lord! Where war-like Ju - das wields his righ - teous

fall thy foes, O Lord! Where war-like Ju - das wields his righ - teous

fall thy foes, O Lord! Where war-like Ju - das wields his righ - teous

fall thy foes, O Lord! Where war-like Ju - das wields his righ - teous

8ves.

sword, Where war-like Ju - das wields his righ - teous sword.

sword, Where war-like Ju - das wields his righ - teous sword.

sword, Where war-like Ju - das wields his righ - teous sword.

sword, Where war-like Ju - das wields his righ - teous sword.

No. **27**   RECIT.—VICTORIOUS HERO.

ISRAELITISH MAN.

VOICE.

Vic - to - rious he - ro! Fame shall tell, With her last breath, how

ACCOMP.

p

A - pol - lo - nius fell; And all Sa - ma - ria fled by thee pur-

- sued Through hills of car - nage and a sea of blood: While

'hy re - sist - less prow - ess dealt a - round, With their own lead - er's

sword, the death - ful wound. Thus, too, the haugh - ty Se - ron, Sy - ria's

boast, Be - fore thee fell, with his un - num - ber'd host.

No. 28   AIR.—SO RAPID THY COURSE IS.

No. 29 RECIT.—WELL MAY WE HOPE OUR FREEDOM TO RECEIVE.

Well may we hope our freedom to receive, Such sweet transporting joys thy actions give.

No. 30 DUET.—SION NOW HER HEAD SHALL RAISE.

Si - on now her head shall raise; Tune your harps, Tune your harps, Tune your harps to songs . . . . . of

Chorus (*5 voices*).—TUNE YOUR HARPS.

Trebles unis.

your harps, Si - on now her head, now her

now her head . . . shall raise. . . . . now her

now her head shall raise; . . Tune your harps, . .

now her head, now her head shall raise; . . . . . .

8ves.

head, shall raise: . . . Tune your harps to songs, to songs of praise, . . .

head shall raise; . . . Tune your harps to songs, to songs of praise, . .

. . Tune your harps, . . . Tune your harps to songs, to songs of praise, Tune your

Tune your harps to songs, to songs of praise, . . .

. . Tune your harps to songs of praise.

. . . Tune your harps . . to songs of praise.

harps, . . . your harps to songs of praise.

. . Tune your harps . . to songs of praise.

No. **31**   Recit.—O LET ETERNAL HONOURS CROWN HIS NAME.

ISRAELITISH WOMAN.

VOICE.

O let e - ternal ho-nours crown his name, Ju-das, first worthy

ACCOMP.

p

in the rolls of fame; Say, "He put on the breastplate as a Gi-ant, And

girt his war-like harness a - bout him; In his acts he was like a li-on, And

like a li - on's whelp roar - ing for his prey."

No. **32** AIR.—FROM MIGHTY KINGS HE TOOK THE SPOIL.

Ju-dah re-joi - - - - - - ceth, re-joi-ceth in his

name, And triumphs, and triumphs in her he-ro's

fame, Ju - dah re - joi - - - - - -

- - - - - ceth, re-joi-ceth in his name,

And triumphs, And triumphs in her he-ro's fame,

And tri-umphs in . . . her he - ro's fame.

Allegro.

Da Capo.

No. **33** Duet.—HAIL, JUDEA, HAPPY LAND!

No. **34** Chorus.—HAIL, JUDEA, HAPPY LAND.

No. **35** Recit.—THANKS TO MY BRETHREN.

No. **36**   Air.—HOW VAIN IS MAN WHO BOASTS IN FIGHT.

How vain   is man   who boasts   in fight

The va-lour of gi - gan - - tic might, The

va - lour of gi - gan - - - - - - - tic

might;   How vain   is man who boasts in fight, who boasts   in fight,   who-

vain is man who boasts . . in fight, . . who boasts . . in fight, The

valour of gi - gan - - - - tic might, The va - lour of gi - gan - -

- - - - - - - - - - - tic might, The

va - - - - lour of gi - gan - tic might.

Fine.

No. **37**   Recit.—O JUDAS! O MY BRETHREN.

sa-cri-fice   To great An-ti-o-chus.   From the E-gyp-tian coast   (Where

Pto-le-my   hath Mem-phis and Pe-lu-sium lost)   He sends the va-liant

Gor-gias,   and commands   His proud vic-to-rious bands   To

root out Israel's strength, and to e-rase Ev'-ry me-mo-rial   of the sacred place.

No. **38**   AIR.—AH! WRETCHED ISRAEL.

LARGO.

p

Violoncello Solo.

Ah! wretched,

(Voice alone.)

CHORUS.—AH! WRETCHED ISRAEL!

No. 40 RECIT.—BE COMFORTED.

No. **41**   Air.—THE LORD WORKETH WONDERS.

- - - - ders, His glo-ry to raise, And still as He thun - - -

- - - ders, And still as He thunders, Is fear-ful in praise, And

still as He thunders, Is fear - ful in praise.

No. 42 Recit.—MY ARMS! AGAINST THIS GORGIAS WILL I GO.

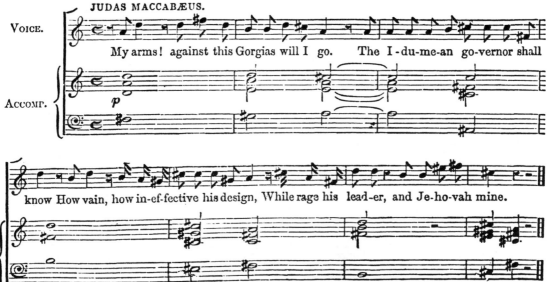

JUDAS MACCABÆUS.

Voice.

My arms! against this Gorgias will I go. The I-du-me-an go-vernor shall

Accomp.

know How vain, how in-ef-fective his design, While rage his lead-er, and Je-ho-vah mine.

No. **43** Air.—SOUND AN ALARM.

Sound an alarm, Sound an alarm, your sil-ver trumpets sound, And

call the brave, and on - ly . . brave, and on - ly brave a - round, call the

brave, call the brave, And on - ly brave a - round.

Sound an a-larm, Your sil - ver trumpets sound, your trumpets

sound, your trumpets sound, And call the brave, and on - ly . . brave, And

call the brave, and on - ly . . brave, And on - ly brave, a - round, call the

brave, call the brave, ...

. . . and on - ly brave, a - round.

Who listeth fol - low; To the field a - gain. Justice with courage,

is a . . . thou-sand men, is a thousand men, Justice with cou-rage, Justice with

cou-rage is a thou-sand men, is a thousand men, is a thou - sand men.

No 43
(Continued.)

AIR.—SOUND AN ALARM!

Chorus.—WE HEAR.

No. 44 RECIT.—ENOUGH: TO HEAV'N WE LEAVE THE REST.

mine. For Si-on, ho-ly Si-on, seat of God, In ruinous heaps is by the heathen

trod. Such profanation calls for swift redress, If e'er in battle Is-rael hopes success.

No. 45 AIR.—WITH PIOUS HEARTS.

LARGHETTO. *mp*

With pi-ous hearts, and brave as pi-ous,

O Si-on, we thy call at - - tend,

cres.

With pi-ous hearts, and brave as pi-ous, and brave as pi-ous, O Si-on,

No. **46**   RECIT.—YE WORSHIPPERS OF GOD.

throng, Wild with de-lusion, pay their nightly song To Ashtoreth, y-clept the Queen of Heav'n;

Hence to Phœnicia be the goddess driv'n; Or be she, with her priests and pageants, hurl'd To the re-

-mo-test cor-ner of the world, Ne'er to de-lude us more with pi-ous lies.

No 47   Air.—WISE MEN FLATT'RING, MAY DECEIVE YOU.

Larghetto.

Wise men ... flatt'ring, may de - - ceive you With their vain .. mys -

- te - rious .. art, With their vain mys - te - rious art;

Ma - gic .. charms can ne'er re - lieve you, Nor can

heal the . . wound-ed heart. No! Ma - gic charms can ne'er re -

- lieve you, Ma - gic .. charms can ne'er re - lieve you, Nor can heal the .

... wounded heart, can - not heal the wound - ed heart.

But true .. wis - dom

can re - lieve you, God - like wis - dom from a - bove, God - like

wis - dom from a - bove; This a - lone can ne'er de - ceive you,

This a - - lone can ne'er de - ceive you, This a - lone all pains re - move.

Dal Segno.

No. **48**   DUET.—OH! NEVER BOW WE DOWN.

ne-ver, ne-ver bow we down, ne-ver, ne-ver bow we down, Oh! never, nev-er

down, ne-ver, ne-ver bow we down, no, no,

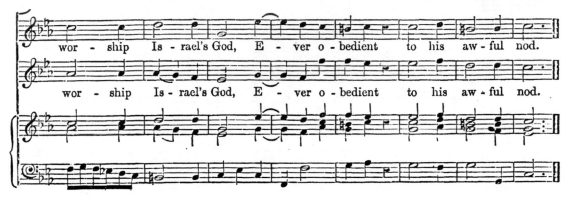

bow we down to the rude stock or sculp-tur'd stone; But e-ver

ne-ver, ne-ver bow we down To the rude stock or sculp-tur'd stone; But e-ver

wor - ship Is - rael's God, E - ver o - bedient to his aw-ful nod.

wor - ship Is - rael's God, E - ver o - bedient to his aw-ful nod.

No. **49** CHORUS.—WE NEVER WILL BOW DOWN.

CANTO.

We ne - - ver will bow down, We ne - ver will bow

ALTO.

We ne - ver, ne - ver will bow down, We ne - ver, ne - ver

TENOR.
(8ve lower.)

We ne - ver, ne - ver will bow down,

BASS.

We ne - ver, ne - ver will bow down, We ne - ver, ne - ver

ACCOMP.

mf

8ves.

131

lone, and God a-lone, We worship God, and God a-lone, and God.. a-

lone, and God a-lone, We worship God, and God a-lone, and God.. a-

lone, and God a-lone, We worship God, and God a-lone, and God.. a-

lone, and God a-lone, We worship God, and God a-lone, and God a-

8ves.

lone, We worship God, we wor - - - - - - ship God,

lone, We worship God, we wor - - - - - ship

lone. We worship God, we wor - - ship

lone. We worship God, we wor - - - - - ship

8ves.

.. and God a-lone, We wor-ship God and God a-lone.

God, and God a-lone, We wor-ship God, and God.. a-lone.

God, and God a-lone, We wor-ship God, and God.. a-lone.

God, and God a-lone, We wor-ship God, and God.. a-lone

END OF THE SECOND PART.

PART THE THIRD.

No. 50   AIR.—FATHER OF HEAV'N.

ANDANTE
LARGHETTO.

Fa - - ther of Heav'n,

(*Voice alone.*)

Fa - ther of Heav'n! from thy e - ter-nal throne, from thy e - ter - nal throne,

Look with an eye   of bless - ing down,   While we pre - pare . . . .

. . . with ho-ly rites, To so-lemn - nize . . . the Feast of Lights.

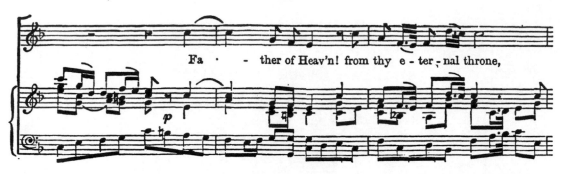

Fa · · ther of Heav'n! from thy e · ter · nal throne,

Look with an eye of bless-ing down, While we pre-

Voice alone.

--pare, ... with ho - ly rites, To so - lem - nize . .

. . . . the Feast of Lights, the Feast of Lights, To

solemn-nize . . . . the Feast of Lights, While we prepare with

ho - ly rites, To so-lem-nize . . . . the Feast of Lights.

And thus our

(Voice alone.)

grate - ful hearts em - ploy; And in thy praise

This al - tar raise, With ca - rols of triumphant joy, This al - tar

raise With carols of triumphant joy, ... With ca - rols of tri -

-um - phant joy. Fa - ther of Heav'n! from

(Voice alone.)

thy e - ternal throne, from thy e - ter - nal throne, Look with an eye of blessing

(Voice alone.)

down; While we pre - pare . . . . with ho - ly rites To

so - lem - nize . . . . the Feast of Lights, the Feast of

Lights, To so - lem - nize . . . . . the Feast of Lights.

No. 52   Recit.—SEE, SEE, YON FLAMES.

ISRAELITISH MAN.

See, see, yon flames that from the al - tar broke, In spi-ry streams pur-

sue the trail-ing smoke; The fragrant incense mounts the yield-ing air,

Sure pre-sage that the Lord hath heard our pray'r.

No. 53   Recit.—O GRANT IT, HEAV'N.

ISRAELITISH WOMAN.

O grant it, Heav'n, that our long woes may cease, And Judah's daughters

taste the calm of peace; Sons, brothers, husbands, to be - wail no

more, Tor - tur'd at home, or ha - vock'd in the war.

No. **54**   AIR.—SO SHALL THE LUTE AND HARP AWAKE.

So shall the lute and harp awake, And sprightly voice sweet des-cant run,

So   shall the   lute a - wake,   So

shall the   harp a - wake,   So shall   the   lute   and harp a - wake, And

In the pure strains,

. . . . In the pure strains of Jes - se's son.

_mf_

_p_

So shall the lute a - wake, So shall the harp a - wake, So

shall the lute and harp a - wake, And spright - ly voice sweet des - cant run, And

spright - ly voice sweet des - - cant run, And spright - - -

In the pure strains of Jes - se's Son.

No. 55 RECIT.—FROM CAPHARSALAMA.

ISRAELITISH MESSENGER.

VOICE.

From Ca - phar - sa - la - ma, on ea - gle wings I

ACCOMP.

8ves.

fly, With ti - dings of im - petuous joy! Come Ly - si - as, with his

host ar-ray'd In coat of mail; their mas - sy shields Of gold and brass flash'd

lightning o'er the fields; While the huge tow'r-back'd E - le - phant dis-

- - play'd A hor-rid front; but Ju-das, un-dismay'd, Met, fought, and

van-quish'd all the rage-ful train. Yet more; Ni-ca-nor

lies with thousands slain; The blas-phemous Ni-ca-nor, who defied The living God, and

in his wanton pride A pub-lic monument ordain'd Of vic-to-ries yet ungain'd.

But lo! The con-quer-or comes; and on his spear, To dis-si-pate all fear, He

bears the vaunter's head and hand, That threaten'd de-so-la-tion to the land.

No. **56**   Chorus.—SEE THE CONQU'RING HERO COMES.

DUET, OR CHORUS OF VIRGINS.

See the God-like youth .. ad-vance, Breathe . the

Canto 2do.

See the God-like youth .. ad-vance, Breathe . the

Flutes. *p*

flutes, and lead .. the dance; Myr - - tle wreaths and ro - ses

flutes, and lead .. the dance; Myr - - tle wreaths and ro - ses

twine, To deck .. the he-ro's brow .. di-vine; Myr-tle .. wreaths and

twine, To deck .. the he-ro's brow .. di-vine; Myr-tle .. wreaths and

ro - - ses twine, To deck .. the he-ro's brow .. di-vine.

ro - - ses twine, To deck .. the he-ro's brow di - vine.

Go on to Chorus.

No. **57**　　　　　　　　　　**MARCH.**

No. **58**   Solo and Chorus,—SING UNTO GOD.

CHORUS.

Sing un - to God, and high af - fections raise, To crown this conquest with

Sing un - to God, and high af - fections raise, To crown this conquest with

Sing un - to God, and high af - fections raise, To crown this conquest with

Sing un - to God, and high af - fections raise, To crown this conquest with

CHORUS.

un - mea - sur'd praise, with un - mea - sur'd, with un-mea - sur'd praise, . .

un-mea - sur'd praise, . . . with un - mea - sur'd, with unmea - sur'd praise, . .

un - mea - sur'd praise, with un - mea - sur'd, with unmea - sur'd praise, with

un mea - sur'd praise, ... with

8ves.

Sing un - to God, and

To crown, . .

unmea - sur'd praise, ... To crown, . . . to

unmea - sur'd praise, with un - measur'd praise.

high affections raise, To crown this conquest with un-mea - sur'd praise, . .

To crown, to crown this conquest, To crown . . this conquest with

crown this conquest, To crown . . . . . . this conquest, this

with un - mea - sur'd praise.

un-mea - sur'd praise, To crown this conquest with un - mea - sur'd praise. . .

conquest, To crown . . . . . . this conquest with unmeasur'd praise. . .

O! Sing,

Sing un - to God, sing un - to God, sing un - to God, and

. . . Sing un - to God, sing un - to God, . . . sing un - to

. . . Sing un - to God, sing un - to God, sing un - to God,

Sing un - to God, sing un - to God, and high af - fec-tions raise, and

Ped. 8ves.

No. 59   RECIT.—SWEET FLOW THE STRAINS

AIR.—WITH HONOUR LET DESERT BE CROWN'D.

No. **60**

ANDANTE LARGHETTO.

JUDAS MACCABÆUS.

With honour let de-sert be crown'd, The trumpet ne'er in vain shall sound,

Voice alone.

The trumpet ne'er in vain shall sound, The trumpet ne'er in vain shall sound.

Solo trumpet.

With honour let desert be crown'd,

With honour let desert be crown'd, The trumpet ne'er in vain shall sound, The

Solo.

trumpet ne'er in vain shall sound; But

all - at-ten-tive to alarms, But all - - - - at - ten-tive to alarms, The

willing nations fly to arms, to arms, to arms, And con-quer-ing, or con-quer'd, And

con-quer-ing or conquer'd, claim . . . . the prize, And

con-quer-ing or con - quer'd, claim the prize,

Of hap - py earth, or far more happy skies.

And con-quering or conquer'd, claim, . . and claim the prize, Of

hap - - py earth. or far more hap-py skies, and claim . . the prize of

hap - - py earth, or far more hap - py skies.

No. **61** RECIT.—PEACE TO MY COUNTRYMEN.

No. **62** CHORUS.—TO OUR GREAT GOD.

168

No. **63** Recit.—AGAIN TO EARTH LET GRATITUDE DESCEND.

Again to earth let gra-ti-tude descend. Praiseworthy is our he-ro and our friend. Come, then, my daughters, choi-cest art be-stow, To weave a chap-let for the vic-tor's brow; And in your songs for e-ver be con-fess'd The va-lour that pre-serv'd, The pow'r that bless'd, Bless'd you with hours, that scatter as they fly. Soft, quiet, gen-tle Love, and boundless Joy.

No. **64**   DUET.—O LOVELY PEACE.*

smile . . with wa - vy corn, with wa - vy corn,

And smile . . . with wa - vy

with wa - vy corn, with wavy corn,

corn, with wa - vy corn, with wa - vy corn, with wa-vy corn,

mf

Adagio.

Let fleecy flocks the hills a . dorn, . the hills . . a-dorn, And

Let fleecy flocks the hills adorn, the hills . . a-dorn, And

p

Adagio.

(Voices

smile . . . . with wa - vy corn.

smile . . . . with wa . vy corn.

mf

p

alone.)

Tempo 1mo.

Let the shrill trum-pet cease, nor o - ther sound,

Let the shrill trum-pet cease, Nor

But Na-ture's song - sters wake . . the cheer - - ful

o - ther sound,

morn, nor o - ther sound, nor o - ther sound wake the

But Nature's song - sters wake . . the cheer - - ful morn, the

cheer - ful morn, But Na - ture's songsters wake the cheer - ful

cheer - ful morn, But Na - ture's songsters wake the cheer - ful

No. 65   AIR.—REJOICE, O JUDAH!

Re-joice,   O Ju-dah, and in songs divine,   With

Che-rubim and Seraphim, har-mo-nious join.   Re-joice,   O Ju-dah,   re-

-joice, ...   re-joice, ...   O Ju-dah,   re-joice,   and in

Go on to Chorus.

No. 66   CHORUS.—HALLELUJAH, AMEN.

men, A - - men, A - men. Hal - le - lu - jah, Hal - le - lu-jah, Hal -
- lu - jah, Hal - le - lu - jah, Hal - le - lu - jah, Hal - le - lu-jah, Amen,
- jah, Hal - le - lu jah, . . . Hal - le - - lu - jah, Hal - le - lu - jah,
- le - lu - jah, ... Hal - le - - lu-jah, Hal - le - lu-jah, Amen,
8ves.
- le - - - - lu - jah, Hal - le - lu - jah, A-men, Amen. Hal - le - lu - jah, A -
Amen. Hal-le-lu-jah, A - men.
Hal - le - lu - jah, Amen, Amen. Hal - le - lu - jah, A -
Amen. Hal-le - lu-jah, A - men.
8ves.
- - men. O Ju-dah, re-joice, re - joice, ... re - joice, . . O
O Ju-dah, re-joice, re-joice, re - joice, re-joice, O
- - men, O Ju-dah, re-joice, re - joice, ... re - joice, . . O
O Ju-dah, re-joice, re - joice, ... re - joice, . . O